MOTIVATIONAL
MOMENTS

PURSUING THE DREAM

CHRISTOPHER A. BROOKS

Copyright © 2018 Christopher A. Brooks
All rights reserved.
ISBN 9781791734503

My Prayer for You

Father, I thank You for those who have made the decision to begin this devotional. I pray that whatever stage of life they are in, and wherever they are in their walk with You, that this devotional will bless them and help them to walk in victory and confidence in You. I ask that as they make this book a part of their daily time with You, that You will touch their heart, empower them with inspiration and revelation to fulfil their God-given purpose. I thank You for the victory over fear, guilt and shame; and the new life of freedom, healing, and deliverance You have called them to walk in. Allow this devotional, Lord, to be a tool to help them grow in their faith, their hope, and their courage to pursue Your will for their life. And I declare and decree, their best is yet to come. In Jesus mighty name. Amen.

Acknowledgements

To my wife and business partner, Tiffany. Thank you for not allowing me to give up on this project, and forever being my number one fan. I love you more than words could ever explain.

To my parents, Willie and Mary Brooks. Thank you for the godly example you have always been in my life. Dad, I finally did it!

To all the spiritual leaders who have groomed me throughout my life. There are too many for me to name, but, yes, I am taking about YOU. I am who I am because God placed you in my life.

Introduction

I was born and raised on the east end of Charleston, West Virginia in a Christian home and family with a lot of love and deeply rooted faith in God despite having to overcome a car accident that almost took the life of my mother and brother, Kenneth and the agony of losing my brother Jerry to gun violence when he was a teenager. My father was a police officer and my mother was a homemaker. Together, they gave me a life that was rich in not just material things, but in faith, support, love, and commitment to family. My father, Willie Brooks married my mother, Mary Frances Brooks, who at that time had three sons and was living within very humble and limited means. Together, as they grew professionally and spiritually, they created a culture and environment for my brothers and later for me that now as a husband and father, by which I am inspired.

As a kid, I remember growing up pretending I was speaking before masses of people. I would stand on the couch and envision a sea of people hanging on to my every word. My mother gives an account of me as a child "preaching" about drinking and drugs being bad for you. Who knew some twenty-five years later, I would be a minister, motivational speaker, consultant and life coach. Throughout my early adult life, I would work different jobs, get certifications and try different ideas that I thought would make money and give me the normal life I thought I was supposed to live. A lot of my experience was in sales, in which I found myself successful; whether in a call center, a mall retail store or selling cars.

It was not until recently that I began to reflect and see a common denominator in my past jobs. I was successful in places where I could connect with people and use my gift of speech. I realized that I was given a gift to help people see value in products and services. I did not find true happiness and fulfilment until I learned how to take my gift and use it for my life purpose. I thought what I could do in church was different from what I was doing in the sales arena, but it was all the same, just a different message. I was not necessarily showing the value of salvation at Nordstrom, but I was connecting with people, meeting a need and communicating with them in such a way that they were willing to decide to invest in what I was presenting to them: hope.

As time moved on, I met my amazing wife, Tiffany. You will read more about her as we go through this devotional/motivational guide. As an army family that is newly retired, my family and I have been blessed to live in places people only dream of vacationing. Throughout my travels, I have spoken to thousands of people of various ethnicities, and cultural and social status. It all started in Charleston, West Virginia in a big green house on Elizabeth Street with a little boy who had a dream of speaking to the masses.

One day, in talking to my father, he told me, "You need to write a book." Now he had been telling me that for a couple years, and in the past, I would entertain the thought for a week or so, and then I would let it go. But this last time when he said it, it was like he punched me! Tiffany and I were going over these motivational moments that I post on social media, and she said, "You know, this could be your book." Again, the gut punch. My mind was blown. I, however, still needed confirmation.

We were at church one Sunday, and our pastor's wife told the leaders, "Some of you have a book that needs to be written." It was like Mike Tyson was giving me his famous jab to the gut, followed by the uppercut to the chin! I finally gave in, and with a plethora of emotions, I began to write. By far this is the most challenging thing I have ever done, but also one of the most fulfilling. The idea that someone I have never met, or have any prior association with, will be reading my book; the idea of making a connection with countless people around the world through words is an amazing experience. I hope to challenge and inspire you.

The sections of this devotional are inspired by people that have had a significant impact in my life. I am the man that I am today, not because of my own doing, but because of the community of faith-filled believers and leaders that helped mold me from childhood to adulthood, in academics, sports and ministry.

Be Motivated is inspired by my father, Willie Brooks. As I mentioned before, he's been telling me for years, "Boy, you need to write a book. I believe its gonna do somethin' powerful". He never stopped telling me that, no matter what crazy turn my life was taking or what I was doing, he was always motivating me to pursue something I honestly did not think I was skilled enough or smart enough to do. Even while this book was being written and produced, he would get on the phone and ask, "How's that book goin'? I can't wait to get my copy!" His motivation and belief in me helped me through some rough times when I wanted to quit. Thanks, dad, for believing in me.

Be Truthful was inspired by my brother, Kenneth "Mister" Williams Jr. He is the most straight-shooting, no-nonsense, integral man I know. He taught and reminds me to let my yes be yes, and my no be no, regardless of feelings just tell the truth. He says I led him to the Lord when I was a teenager. I remember the conversation and I am just glad that God gives us the boldness and the courage to tell the truth, even when we think our lives might be in jeopardy. He tells me that after I told him like it is, he was angry with me. But while he was in his car, his anger shifted into pride. He was proud of the fact that I stood there (behind mom) and gave him the truth about needing God in his life in order to be the man of his family that God wants him to be. Today, he is an ordained Elder in the Lord's church, international speaker and my personal motivational coach.

Be Wise was inspired by my Bishop, Curtis Lindsey who has gone to be with the Lord. He had a sixteen-year-old kid with a calling to preach the gospel in his face; recognized it and started me on a path of being the spiritual leader I am today. His wisdom taught me kingdom principles such as being a good steward, submission to authority, always being ready to share Gods word with others, loving God's people, and how to guard your heart are just a few.

Be Transparent was inspired by the love of my life, my best friend, mother of our son, Alan and business partner, Tiffany Brooks. Tiffany and I met at a time when I was rebuilding myself after a very emotional and painful divorce. I was in school and just starting a small business (in other words, I was broke) and there was nothing I had to bring to the table. While others told her not to give me a second thought, she saw something in me that, at that time, I did not even see in myself. We married in 2008, and God took us on the adventure of a lifetime. We are "Team Brooks". She has an amazing voice; is highly skilled in dance; writes and is an amazing mother to our children. With so many talents and abilities, along with her spiritual gift of knowledge, she is a force in the Lord's Church. By way of the U.S. Army, God has allowed us to serve God's people in Alaska (Greater Friendly Temple COGIC), Hawaii (Word of Life Christian Center), Italy (Vicenza Gospel Service), and now here in El Paso, Texas (Destiny Family Christian Center).

    Wherever and whenever God gives me the opportunity to preach, teach, go on television, give a talk in a corporate business setting, or give a speech for Toastmasters International, Tiffany always tells me of the importance of transparency. Her encouragement has allowed me to experience a level of freedom I never had before. Being transparent in ministry was very foreign to me. Growing up in church, people did not talk about their struggles or missteps, so I kept things superficial and "churchy". Her message of transparency ripped the veil of pride and fear from my life and now I can share my story from a very healthy and honest place. This book would have never been written if not for her.

    Be Free was inspired by Pastor Perry Kerney. I was in the process of retiring from the Army due to medical reasons, and it was not in my plan. I was freaking out, depressed, scared, yet excited, motivated and ready to start the next chapter of my life. Pastor Kearney is the one who inspired me to get my Life Coaching certification and business started. He helped me see that I did not have to follow the status quo, and just go out and do something. He helped me to really ask myself what it was that I loved, was passionate about and gifted to do. From talks with him, Tiffany and I started The B.E. Group (Brooks Enrichment) and I became a Life Coach, which quickly birthed my public speaking career. Pastor Perry is the person who gave me a phone number to call after I spent fifteen minutes complaining about being in a city where nobody knows me and not knowing how to get my name "out there". After calling that number and speaking to a nice little lady who happened to own a local Christian television station and happened to need someone to host a show the next day! Once I sat in that studio and I saw the light on the camera turn on, I experienced a freedom and a joy that is truly unexplainable. A year later, I'm still there with more to come about television for 2019! I am thankful to Pastor Perry, for his mentorship and friendship.

Be Strong was inspired by a collection of leaders that helped me in my life. I was fortunate throughout my ministry to serve as adjutant or associate pastor to very powerful leaders. Being that close to someone, you see things that everyone else does not get to see. I was blessed to have amazing mentoring moments while driving to a service, or after visiting the sick, and even when putting up drywall to the building that would become the sanctuary for God's people to worship. I have seen leaders on the mountaintops of success and the valleys of despair, all while encouraging others to hold on to God and not to let go. Their strength to maintain and to obey God when, at times, they would have had every reason to quit taught me a lot about leadership and honoring what God has given us.

Be Secure was inspired by Pastor James Reese. Back then, minister Reese had started a youth small group from his home. He and Deacon Kevin Wilborne were the youth leaders at our church, Greater Emmanuel Gospel Tabernacle. We met every Thursday evening, and he is the man that led me to the Lord when I was thirteen years old.

Now, you must understand that I was a new Christian, in a very strict Apostolic Pentecostal church and I was thirteen. I loved God, wanted to live according to the Word of God, but I was also thirteen. With all my insecurities of being this skinny and short kid, I didn't understand how to fit in with my friends and still be a Christian. He spent a lot of time letting me cry and ask, "What's wrong with me?" because I was just different. Pastor Reese taught me to believe the Word of God that says I am fearfully and wonderfully made (Psalm 139:14). He mentored me, discipled me and never judged me. He helped me be secure in who I am, and God has allowed me to mentor others that lack that confidence in their God-given ability.

To this day, he is one of the people I go to and discuss what God is speaking to me and put in my heart. His wife, Kay, told me one day after seeing my bad grades (I just wanted to go to church not school), "God don't need no dummies in his kingdom. Get those grades up." I am sending Kay a personal invitation to my graduation at New Mexico State University.

Be Secure was also inspired by my pastors, Bishop Richard L. Johnson and Co-pastor Adele Johnson. Their love and support for our family is priceless. They are truly an example of God's love for humanity, an excellent example of being secure in God's word, and having integrity and Godly character. I thank God for the blessing the two of them are to the body of Christ!

A lot of love and prayer has gone into this devotional. I pray it will bless you and help you in your spiritual journey. I believe this will be a great resource for people of all ages and stages of life. Are you ready? Let's get started!

MOTIVATIONAL MOMENTS
PURSUING THE DREAM

Week One

Be Secure Sunday

"THIS VISION-MESSAGE IS A WITNESS POINTING TO WHAT'S COMING. IT ACHES FOR THE COMING—IT CAN HARDLY WAIT! AND IT DOES NOT LIE. IF IT SEEMS SLOW IN COMING, WAIT. IT IS ON ITS WAY. IT WILL COME RIGHT ON TIME". **-HABAKKUK 2:2-3 MSG**

What is your dream? If money, education, connections or anything else that is currently a challenge today was no longer an issue, what would your life look like? What would be your way of influencing and inspiring others? How would you help make a difference in the lives of those in need of significant change? Where would you live, what would you do with your time, talents and resources? Your dream is not the result of spicy pizza and milkshakes eaten too late the night before. Your dream is the cry of purpose drawing you out of the darkness of existing and into the light of living a fulfilled life. Whatever your dream is, you must be in relentless pursuit of it, no matter how big or ridiculous or impossible it may seem to be. Being a dreamer is not always the most popular or celebrated position, especially if the dream is beyond the "normal" scope of thinking within your sphere of influence. When your vision defies your status, please do not expect a standing ovation and the keys to the city. Unfortunately, you will often receive the completely opposite response. Everyone will not understand or accept your dream, and if you are not careful, their words and behavior can cause you to halt, prolong, and even abort the dream before it even has a chance to materialize.

    In the Old testament, Joseph had a dream about becoming someone of great power and influence. After sharing his dream with the ones many would think would be excited for him, he was hated, rejected, beaten, cast into a pit and sold into slavery! Although Joseph had to go through many challenging situations, that at times probably felt hopeless, the Bible shows us how he did eventually become that person of influence and power. You and I must ignore the critics, and sometimes even ignore ourselves! It is not the responsibility of others to believe in you. YOU must believe in yourself! It is YOUR dream, YOUR goals, YOUR life purpose and nobody else's. Do not allow the toxic words of small-thinking, faithless people talk you out of your dream. They will cause you to doubt, which in turn produces fear, and births an empty, unfulfilled life. Nothing of value comes without some form of process and testing. Be secure in the promises of God, that whatever he has given you to do; whatever dream He has placed in you will come to pass in its time and season. The key that I have found to help me is to make sure that I am ready before it comes.

    Today, be secure and accept the truth that you deserve the dream that God has given you. You have everything you need to make your dream happen, but you must be courageous enough to get up and do what it takes to make the dream a reality. It might not happen today or next week but continue to be a dreamer. Make the phone calls; write the business plan; create the website; get the education. Everyday do something that gets you closer to your dream.

Surround yourself with other dreamers that will encourage you and speak words of hope and life to you, especially when the days get longer, the calls feel useless, and the book seems to be too large of a task to complete. Will it be easy? No. But will it be worth it when it comes? Yes!

Be Motivated Monday

"WORDS KILL, WORDS GIVE LIFE; THEY'RE EITHER POISON OR FRUIT—YOU CHOOSE." **PROVERBS 18:21 MSG**

When Tiffany and I first started The B.E. Group, people would ask me about the business. Fear would begin to creep in my heart, and I would respond to them saying things like, "OK, don't laugh but...", "It is only" or "I do not claim to be and expert" kind of phrases. I quickly realized, that what I saw in our company, and the vision I had for where we were going, versus what I was saying, was not lining up. In fact, my words were in complete contradiction to the values and mission of The B.E. Group. I was downplaying the value of my dream, because of fear of what others would think or say to me. This came from unresolved issues from my past failures and a sense of not feeling worthy to lay claim to something that will potentially reach lives all over the world; help people live out their life purpose and in turn find fulfillment in being who they have been created to be. I thought, "How can I be someone's coach when I have made so many mistakes in my life over the years? How can I motivate others to dream big when I am fighting the urge to go back to what is familiar and comfortable myself?" This was the conversation I was having with myself, and if you are reading this, you are probably shaking your head because you have been there, as well. Or, maybe you are there right now. If you are, keep reading. Your story is not over, just like mine is not. Keep going but be careful what you say.

Here is the bottom line up front my friend. You can have an amazing dream and have everything in place to succeed. But you will cripple, sabotage and utterly defeat yourself if you minimalize the value of your dream. You have a choice to make today: Do I speak words of life and success to my dream? Or, do I speak death and defeat? Give yourself a fighting chance at success, by speaking life even if others are critical. Get away from dream killers! They live small and want you to reside in their small way of living. Be motivated! Speak to your dream today, and watch it come alive!

Be Truthful Tuesday

"YOU LAZY FOOL... HOW LONG BEFORE YOU GET OUT OF BED? A NAP HERE, A NAP THERE, A DAY OFF HERE, A DAY OFF THERE, SIT BACK, TAKE IT EASY—DO YOU KNOW WHAT COMES NEXT? JUST THIS: YOU CAN LOOK FORWARD TO A DIRT-POOR LIFE, WITH POVERTY YOUR PERMANENT HOUSEGUEST!" **PROVERBS 6:6-11 MSG**

One of the most deceiving, dream-killing tricks that we often fall for is procrastination. All of us have been guilty of this in some way, shape or form. The truth is, my book would have been finished months ago, I would be in a corporate office building instead of my home office, and I would have a PhD right now if I did not fall into procrastination. You were created to be great and to live a life that brings glory to God and honor to your family. You have the capacity to excel in anything you set your mind to do. But none of these inherent acts of genius can be brought to fruition if procrastination resides in the corner of your mind. We must overcome it.

One of the biggest traps I have experienced and try to help others avoid, is procrastination through prolonged preparation. I would "prepare" to do something for so long, the task would eventually be forgotten, and nothing was ever actually accomplished. You may have family members like this. They come to the family dinner or the family reunion with the big announcement that they are going to be a fashion stylist! Last month they were going to be a respiratory technician. Last Thanksgiving, they announced they were going to be a vending machine mogul. The presentation of what they had planned to do might have been surprisingly good. And maybe for a week (I am being nice) they started off strong, until the reality that the dream does not just float out of the clouds with the heavenly choir singing. There is a harsh reality that whatever you are going after in life is going to take work. It is going to cause some late nights and early mornings. It is going to take weekends of working, making calls and having meetings.

Procrastination is for the weak. It is for daydreamers who just talk big but they are not being truthful to themselves, or to others. Be truthful with yourself and with others when discussing the dream you plan to advance. When preparing, take an honest assessment of the work and sacrifice that will be needed, then make your plan to succeed despite the challenges. Anything that has significant value must go through a process, some fire, some chaos for the best of it to come forth. Procrastination is a cancer that eats away at the value and importance your dream. With each unproductive minute that goes by, procrastination is eating away at your time, your energy and your focus. It kills all the vital behaviors necessary for success in any endeavor. You must be truthful within yourself and find the root behind your procrastination. Is it fear, unforgiveness, financial strains? Is it doubting your ability or God's ability? Once you find the root of it, say what Barney Fife said on the Andy Griffith show, "Nip it, nip it, nip it, in the bud." Your future is too great to let this cancer eat away your potential. Stay focused this week on your dream and let's overcome procrastination.

Be Wise Wednesday

"BUT AS FOR YOU, BE STRONG AND DO NOT GIVE UP, FOR YOUR WORK WILL BE REWARDED." **2 CHRONICLES 15:7 NIV**

Do not give up on your dream. You will have challenges and failures on the way to your dream. That does not disqualify you from being who you were created to be. In my early adulthood, I knew I wanted to be married one day. I wanted what my parents and my brother had. My parents have been happily married for over forty years, and my brother has been married to his wife for over twenty years. I was blessed to have good examples of loving relationships, men that were providers, and how blended families can thrive and be drama free. What I did not see was the pain of two divorces and being a single mother with three boys. I did not see my brother being a stepfather and father figure to my nephew and a family friend's son. Raising them newly married and dealing with strikes, puberty, girl issues, boy issues, and everything in between.

To see them today, you would never think this is the story of my family. What both couples showed me was commitment, perseverance and faith. Whatever your dream is, it is going to come with a price. It is going to have a testimony of overcoming attached to it. Quitting is easy. Cheating is easy. Dropping out is easy. Success takes work. If you are willing to persevere through the storms that will blow in your life, you are on the right course for success in every area of your life. The payoff of wisdom through perseverance is success. If you do not believe me, check this out:

- Bill Gates' first business failed.
- Albert Einstein did not speak until age four.
- Jim Carrey used to be homeless.
- Benjamin Franklin dropped out of school at age ten.
- Stephen King's first book was rejected thirty times!
- Oprah's first boss told her she was too emotional and not right for television.
- Jay-Z could not get signed to any record labels.
- Steven Spielberg was rejected from USC, twice.

What will history say about you?

Be Transparent Thursday

"THEN YOU WILL EXPERIENCE FOR YOURSELVES THE TRUTH, AND THE TRUTH WILL FREE YOU"- **JOHN 8:31-32 MSG**

  Transparency is showing the true you. It is showing others the freedom of knowing how to just be. It is the ultimate liberator because you should never worry about people understanding you. You should never worry about being called a fake or a phony or being threatened to be exposed. When you live your life being transparent, people cannot threaten certain levels of exposure against you. To hold your true self captive in chains of fake smiles and empty conversation, is a life of bondage and emotional torment.

  Until recently, I had this habit of only calling my parents and only talking about the good stuff going on. I would talk to my mentor and only tell him about all the progress The B.E. Group was making. Although, what I was telling them was the truth, I was still lacking total honesty. I did not tell them I had such a horrific anxiety attack that I was moments from being hospitalized. I did not tell them I was struggling with the pressure of financing a business out of my own pocket while also maintaining a home. I only gave them the fluff. If you truly want to thrive in life and have healthy relationships and a successful ministry or business, you must find the strength to be transparent. I was highlighting the dream while hiding my personal nightmares. The freedom I have now came the day I realized my mentor is not just there to talk about success, but to be present when I am struggling emotionally, spiritually, financially, etc. I had to understand my father and mother were already proud of me, so I did not have to put that kind of pressure on myself trying to earn their love. Today declare, "My dream is real. My faith is strong. Today is my chance to be great!"

Be Free Friday

"IT WAS GOOD FOR ME TO BE AFFLICTED SO THAT I COULD LEARN YOUR STATUTES" **PSALM 119:71 CSB**

    All great comeback stories have one thing in common. They all had a setback or failure to come back from! You will not grow nor learn in life until you first become free to fail. Once you fail, and see what caused it, you officially have become wiser and now can implement the necessary changes. Henry Ford had five failed businesses before he founded Ford Motor Company. I failed the promotion board and college the first time. I could have chosen to give up but, instead, I studied harder and made sure I was better prepared. Not only did I get the promotion I sought, I earned my associate's degree.

    Being great is not a result of a fail free life. It is the result of using failure as a springboard to propel you towards your destiny. Be relentless in your pursuit of greatness; do not let anything, anybody or any failure stop you. Be free today even if things do not work the first, second, fifteenth or twentieth time! Let that still small voice that's saying, "one more time" ring loud enough to make you get up and go after your dream!

Be Strong Saturday

"...THOUGH IT TARRY, WAIT FOR IT; BECAUSE IT WILL SURELY COME, IT WILL NOT TARRY" **HABAKKUK 2:3 KJV**

"ALL OUR DREAMS CAN COME TRUE, IF WE HAVE THE COURAGE TO PURSUE THEM." **WALT DISNEY**

I wrote this poem one morning while preparing a motivational moment. I began to think about how people who have made significant marks in our world were just ordinary people like you and me. Make the time you have in this life count for something. Whose life will you effect for the better? What words will you say that will linger in the hearts of others for years to come. Dare to dream big! If someone asks you why are you dreaming such large, lavish, expansive dreams, ask them why not?

Why not dream of owning something that does not exist yet? Why not pursue a PHD even though you have a GED? (Dr. Bon Blossom)
Why not dream to hold the highest office in the land? Even though you're a brotha from the Southside, right arm up with a fisted hand. (President Barack Obama)
Why not have a TV show, books and a magazine in your name? You went through the fire to get there, so OWN that which you have made. (Oprah Winfrey)
Why not be America's favorite preacher, a gatherer of millions and spiritual father to many? When your past had you in the West Virginia hills in obscurity. (Bishop TD Jakes)
Why not open that business with nothing but a dream and a prayer? Grind and scrape young man or woman, and you soon will get there. (Christopher Brooks)

You see, dreams do come true to those who refuse to stop. So, hold on, keep going and be relentless in your approach to your dream! Success is not prejudiced or jealous of your potential to be great. It does not hold grudges or look at your past mistakes. Success makes itself available to everyone and anyone who is willing to pursue it. It is a choice we all must make, and a journey to which we must dedicate our life. Success is not a place to get to, it is a mindset, a language, a culture that is lived daily.

MOTIVATIONAL MOMENTS
PURSUING THE DREAM

Week Two

Be Secure Sunday

"AND LET US NOT NEGLECT OUR MEETING TOGETHER, AS SOME PEOPLE DO, BUT ENCOURAGE ONE ANOTHER, ESPECIALLY NOW THAT THE DAY OF HIS RETURN IS DRAWING NEAR." **HEBREWS 10:25 NLT**

    I grew up in a strict Apostolic Pentecostal church in Charleston, West Virginia. Growing up in a small town, in a family of preachers, pastors and singers, church was a major part of my life. My entire childhood was structured around the church experience. I was in the children's choir, and as a teenager I was the youngest member of the adult choir. I taught myself how to tie a full Windsor knot and by sixteen, I was a licensed minister. Today, I have learned how to balance family, church, and business (ok I am still working on it), but most importantly, having a genuine relationship with Jesus is our foundation.

    To be a finisher, you need a good foundation, a starting point towards fulfilling your life purpose. The church is a great place to make your start. The church is not limited to a building; that is just a location. The church is within you. As a community of believers, we come together to be encouraged, strengthened and energized to go back to our communities and be a light to a dying world. Being connected to a local church, allows you to serve and honor God as you fulfil your life purpose. You do not have to be perfect, but you can be secure in knowing God loves you and will perfect whatever He begins in you. Get connected to a local church and begin your journey of purpose.

Be Motivated Monday

"THEREFORE, SINCE WE ARE SURROUNDED BY SO GREAT A CLOUD OF WITNESSES [WHO BY FAITH HAVE TESTIFIED TO THE TRUTH OF GOD'S ABSOLUTE FAITHFULNESS], STRIPPING OFF EVERY UNNECESSARY WEIGHT AND THE SIN WHICH SO EASILY AND CLEVERLY ENTANGLES US, LET US RUN WITH ENDURANCE AND ACTIVE PERSISTENCE THE RACE THAT IS SET BEFORE US," HEBREWS **12:1 AMP**

I am motivated to be my message. I want to be a finisher. I have multiple things to accomplish like getting my content published, hosting workshops and conferences, and motivating people all over the world to dream big and live their best life. My first goal was to finish this first book before starting other writing projects.

The race you are running is yours alone. The fulfilment of the dreams, passion and purpose for which you are reaching is not the responsibility of anyone else, only you. I have allowed fear, excuses and small thinking to hinder me in my life. While it is easy and a little less painful to handle when you can find others to point the finger at, when it comes to this race of endurance, you are not competing against anyone except yourself. Determine today that you will get out of your own way and be.

Be Truthful Tuesday

"I AM NOT SAYING THAT I HAVE THIS ALL TOGETHER, THAT I HAVE IT MADE. BUT I AM WELL ON MY WAY, REACHING OUT FOR CHRIST, WHO HAS SO WONDROUSLY REACHED OUT FOR ME..." **PHILIPPIANS 3:12MSG**

Growing up in the church, I perfected the very bad habit of wearing a mask to keep people in a safe place. My mask consisted of a lot of jokes, big smiles and even by using my spiritual gift of exhortation. I was full of insecurities, fear and an unhealthy need to be accepted. When I started preaching at age sixteen, I really felt the need to appear that I had everything together. The leaders in our church and organization always seemed to be so well polished and put together. I thought that was how they were all the time. I did not have anyone to explain to me that these spiritual "super heroes" were just regular men and women that had struggles and flaws just like the rest of us. It was not until much later in life, and after falling on my face and being humbled more times than I care to remember, that I realized that I was my worst enemy. I was putting so much pressure on myself trying to live up to an image that really did not exist or matter. Jesus is the perfect example of someone that had temptations, challenges, and His fair share of highs and lows, all while being the Son of God! We must be willing to be transparent and let others know that we all have struggles and failures and that we are all recipients of the grace of God. None of us are perfect. We are all a work in progress! I have made bad decisions, had failed relationships and even been homeless! So, when I tell you that God can take you from a place of hopelessness to a life full of purpose and peace, I say it from a very real and personal place. That is why I decided to write this devotional; to give you, the reader, a message of hope and encouragement to live your best life. Life plus our choices outside of God equals pain, stress, sickness, and death. However, life in Christ plus His word equals joy, peace, health, and an abundant life!

Be Wise Wednesday

"BECOME WISE BY WALKING WITH THE WISE; HANG OUT WITH FOOLS AND WATCH YOUR LIFE FALL TO PIECES," **PROVERBS 13:20 MSG**

I remember my youth leader and mentor, Pastor James Reese, took me to a basketball hoop on the east end of Charleston, WV where I grew up. I was a teenager living for the Lord but struggling with my identity and self-esteem. I was short, skinny and I wore these big glasses (it was the 90's). I was so upset because as much as I liked playing basketball, I was told it was a tall person's game, and I honestly just did not have the skills to play well. In my mind, at the time, it was just validating the self-defeating mindset I had about myself of being less than, insignificant and worthless. Pastor Reese let me cry, and once that was over, he put the ball in my hand and made me dribble, and dribble and dribble some more. Right hand, left hand, crossing from left to right. I was thinking, "When do I get to shoot?" He later had me do layups from the right and then the left. By the end of that time with him I was dribbling and shooting with confidence.

I later ended up playing on teams while in the Air Force and helped coach younger leagues. I now play when I have the time, and I remember those fundamentals he taught me so long ago. He helped me to accomplish my dream of being able to play basketball well, and, to this day, we laugh and talk about that moment. What is your dream? What are you striving to become? Whatever your dream is, find someone that is already doing it, and doing it well. My mentor is thriving in his coaching practice. He has more clients than he has time. I pull from his experience and I am inspired by his success. Let the haters continue to live small. Dream big and learn from someone who is living what you are dreaming.

Be Transparent Thursday

"THEREFORE, EACH OF YOU MUST PUT OFF FALSEHOOD AND SPEAK TRUTHFULLY TO YOUR NEIGHBOR, FOR WE ARE ALL MEMBERS OF ONE BODY."
EPHESIANS 4:25 NIV

Whenever Tiffany and I and the boys go home to Charleston to visit my family, it is always a time we can just be. My brother, Kenneth aka "Mister" and sister in-law, Roz, do not see a motivational speaker, Army veteran, elder, or any other title I hold. I am just Chris, Mister's baby brother. Having people in your life that allow you to be your true self, is a priceless asset. Pursuing your dream will make you wear many different hats. As you start reaching levels of success and accomplishment, you will find people who will want to attach themselves to your success. Some can see the potential and path of where you are going, and they will want to be connected to you. I have been asked to sit on several boards and partner with many businesses that have great potential, resources and an amazing vision. I had to learn that I cannot be everywhere all the time.

It feels great to feel wanted or needed. It is nice to hear people speak highly of you and the work you do. But my mother shared a nugget of wisdom with me that I want to share with you right now. She said, "You have to hear them but do not hear them". In other words, it is nice to hear the praises of people, but If you are not careful, it can go to your head. You can easily lose focus and a sense of who you are.

You need people that will keep you grounded, and will encourage you to take off the hat, the mask and feel free to be transparent.

Be Free Friday

"THEREFORE IF ANYONE IS IN CHRIST [THAT IS, GRAFTED IN, JOINED TO HIM BY FAITH IN HIM AS SAVIOR], HE IS A NEW CREATURE [REBORN AND RENEWED BY THE HOLY SPIRIT]; THE OLD THINGS [THE PREVIOUS MORAL AND SPIRITUAL CONDITION] HAVE PASSED AWAY. BEHOLD, NEW THINGS HAVE COME [BECAUSE SPIRITUAL AWAKENING BRINGS A NEW LIFE]" **2 CORINTHIANS 5:17 AMP**

I was making a lot of money at a young age and living the dream. I had the house, cars and everything else that comes with worldly success. I chose to live beyond my means and made excuses for spending foolishly. Nobody could tell me anything, because I felt that I earned it; it was honest money, and it brought no harm to anyone. It was literally like having a prodigal son experience. Over time, the money went away and so did everything I thought was stable in my life. Thank God for second chances! I prayed and told God that if He would give me another chance at success, that I would keep Him first and honor Him with it.

God has given me another chance, and I am doing my part to honor Him in all that I do with our company. The choices we make may cause us to fall or fail. Do not allow the guilt of past mistakes to bind you and make you feel that there is no hope for a comeback. You must make the choice to be free from shame and past hurts to receive all the blessings that are rightfully yours. God makes all things new. It is a new day, a new opportunity and a new start towards your dream coming to fruition. Your comeback is determined by your choice to change. Be free and never look back!

Be Strong Saturday

"WHEN HE CAME TO HIS SENSES, HE SAID, 'HOW MANY OF MY FATHER'S HIRED SERVANTS HAVE FOOD TO SPARE, AND HERE I AM STARVING TO DEATH! I WILL SET OUT AND GO BACK TO MY FATHER AND SAY TO HIM: FATHER, I HAVE SINNED AGAINST HEAVEN AND AGAINST YOU. I AM NO LONGER WORTHY TO BE CALLED YOUR SON; MAKE ME LIKE ONE OF YOUR HIRED SERVANTS.' SO HE GOT UP AND WENT TO HIS FATHER. "BUT WHILE HE WAS STILL A LONG WAY OFF, IIIS FATHER SAW HIM AND WAS FILLED WITH COMPASSION FOR HIM; HE RAN TO HIS SON, THREW HIS ARMS AROUND HIM AND KISSED HIM." **LUKE 15:17-20 NIV**

Being strong does not mean that you have done everything right and every decision you have made was a good one. Failing is part of the process to greatness. People who try to live their life without failures never really accomplish anything of true significance. Just because something has never been done, does not mean it cannot be done. I must be careful of who I talk to about some of the things Tiffany and I plan to do with our company and for our personal goals, because some people cannot handle the magnitude of our dream. The fear of failure will cripple you and most importantly the fear of not being able to recover will stop you in your tracks. Whether it is failure while attempting to reach a goal, or failure from bad life choices, Gods love for you is there to heal and recover. Guilt is a weapon the devil uses to keep us from turning back to God. You must be strong enough to "come to yourself" and realize that although you have fallen, that is not where you belong. You were born for greatness; your identity is hidden in Christ, and He makes all things new. Even though you may have failed in relationships or at a business venture, it does not make you a failure. Those failures become the resistance necessary to build your strength up, so you can carry the weight of responsibility that comes with success. Get up; brush yourself off; keep going and BE STRONG!

MOTIVATIONAL MOMENTS
PURSUING THE DREAM

Week Three

Be Secure Sunday

"THIS VISION-MESSAGE IS A WITNESS POINTING TO WHAT'S COMING. IT ACHES FOR THE COMING—IT CAN HARDLY WAIT! AND IT DOES NOT LIE. IF IT SEEMS SLOW IN COMING, WAIT. IT IS ON ITS WAY. IT WILL COME RIGHT ON TIME." **HABAKKUK 2:2-3 MSG**

What are you dreaming about? Whatever your dream is, you must determine to be in relentless pursuit of your dream. Everyone will not understand or accept your dream, but you must ignore the critics and sometimes ignore yourself! Do not allow what, small thinking, faithless, people say about your dream. They cause you to doubt your ability to have your dream come true. Be Secure and accept the fact that you deserve that dream, and God almighty wouldn't have given it to you if you couldn't ever achieve it. You have everything you need inside of you to make your dream happen, but you must be courageous enough to dream big. It might not happen today or next week but be a dreamer. Every day do something that gets you closer to your dream. Make the phone calls, write the business plan, create the website, etc. Surround yourself with dreamers that will encourage you when the days get longer, and the calls feel useless and the book seems to be too large of a task to complete. Will it be easy? No. But will it be worth it when it comes to pass? Yes!

Be Motivated Monday

"THIS IS THE DAY WHICH THE LORD HATH MADE; WE WILL REJOICE AND BE GLAD IN IT." **PSALMS 118:24 KJV**

I used to dread Mondays. I always felt like, "Here we go! I wonder what is going to go wrong today for the Monday curse." Tiffany always tells me to choose my attitude. How you view today or anything else in life is all determined by the attitude you choose to have about it. Choose to speak life and love to whatever meeting you must attend, interview you have, phone calls that must be made or classes you must attend. Your attitude will make a world of difference. It is Monday, so choose your attitude and determine that today will be full of opportunities, progress, connections and growth. Be motivated to get out there and own your day.

Be Truthful Tuesday

"AND YE SHALL KNOW THE TRUTH, AND THE TRUTH SHALL MAKE YOU FREE." **JOHN 8:32 KJV**

      Martin Luther King Jr once said, "I believe that unarmed truth and unconditional love will have the final word." There are a lot of things in life that have facts attached to it. It is a medical fact that I have Post Traumatic Stress Disorder (PTSD). It is a fact that you may have loved ones with a sickness or know someone that has been laid off from a job. These are facts based on undeniable evidence. But the facts do not have the final say for those whose hope and faith are in Christ. Jesus said in John 8:32, "You shall know the truth, and the truth shall make you free". Facts may say I have PTSD, but the truth is by Jesus' wounds on Calvary's cross I am healed. Facts may say your loved one has been laid off, but the truth is my God shall supply all of your needs according to His riches in glory (Philippians 4:19). Today, choose to be truthful and speak the word of truth over the situational facts. Things are always subject to change, you just must decide when you want them to change. Your victory has already been won. When Jesus died on the cross iand rose again on the third day, His victory became our victory. Whatever struggle you may be going through, its no match for the victory you have been given through Christ. Make the choice to speak the truth about who you are. You are healed, delivered, and free. You are the redeemed of the Lord!

Be Wise Wednesday

"CONVINCED OF THIS, I KNOW THAT I WILL REMAIN, AND I WILL CONTINUE WITH ALL OF YOU FOR YOUR PROGRESS AND JOY IN THE FAITH." **PHILIPPIANS 1:25 NIV**

This verse is really the heartbeat of our company. I often ask business owners what it is that we can do to help promote their progress. It takes them by surprise because it is not the common narrative in today's business world. Typically, it is about what I can get from somebody else to help me advance my efforts. I have learned through the word of God, experience and observation, that when you support and celebrate someone else's ministry, business, endeavors, God honors that and will bless you. It takes humility, maturity and honesty to help someone else achieve their dream. Who can you help? Into whom are you willing to invest time, talent or treasure? The blessing is in the giving of yourself. When they win, we all win!

Be Transparent Thursday

"FOR HIS INVISIBLE ATTRIBUTES, NAMELY, HIS ETERNAL POWER AND DIVINE NATURE, HAVE BEEN CLEARLY PERCEIVED, EVER SINCE THE CREATION OF THE WORLD, IN THE THINGS THAT HAVE BEEN MADE. SO, THEY ARE WITHOUT EXCUSE." **ROMANS 1:20 ESV**

    A synonym for the word transparent is "undisguised". Growing up, I was always the shortest kid in the bunch. When it came to playing team sports, I was always last to be picked, and of course no one wants to be the last person picked on the team. It hurt my feelings every time but being a kid on the east side of Charleston, I could not go around crying because I was the last to be picked. So, I learned over time to just get in the game and do my part to show that I deserved to be on the team. That behavior carried into my adult life. I wore a disguise of laughter, turning everything into a joke, and living in fear of what people thought of me.

    The same way I had to ask God to heal the pain I had harbored for so many years, you might have to do that as well. What disguise do you wear? Is Facebook the disguise you use to display what you think social media world wants to see. Is your daily status the person you want to be, or the person you think will get you a lot of "likes"? Do we post Bible verses, pictures of money or pictures of food to show people that anyone's life can turn around and be better than how they started? Or, is it to show people a lifestyle you have staged to keep people from getting in your business?

I decided to be the change and launch a business that thrives off of transparency. People need to know that every day is not a great day, and you are not sure how tomorrow is going to look! Your journey to being great does not come without a story of pain and struggle sometimes. That is why we try to limit our exposure to phony people. Phony people are the worst because they are bound. They choose to live a lie and in living a lie they walk around stressed trying to nurse the lie they have birthed. Be the change; decide to be transparent and watch the people God will put in your life that will experience relief and comfort in knowing they are not as awkward as they feel.

Your transparency very well could be the deciding factor of that kid, teen, single mom, alcoholic, drug addict, weak Christian or fallen preacher committing suicide, or deciding to live and start loving the greatness that is in them. Be transparent today, and WIN!

Be Free Friday

"LIVE AS FREE PEOPLE, BUT DO NOT USE YOUR FREEDOM AS A COVER OR PRETEXT FOR EVIL, BUT [USE IT AND LIVE] AS BOND-SERVANTS OF GOD."
1 PETER 2:16 AMP

The movie, *12 Years a Slave*, is set years before the Civil War. Solomon Northup (Chiwetel Ejiofor), a free black man from upstate New York, is kidnapped and sold into slavery in the South. In the 12th year of this ordeal, a chance meeting with an abolitionist from Canada changes Solomon's life forever. Like the movie, I was a slave to my thoughts, many years ago, when I was a young minister in the church. I allowed myself to think that reaching people was in how loud I could get. If there was an organ backing me up, so I could tune up (black churches know what that means), and if I jumped on a pew, it was over. Now God would bless the people, and we did have divine moments. But, when I did not do all of that, and the people would sit quietly on the edge of their seats, and write every word I said, and would flood the altar for prayer, I would cry in the back feeling like a complete failure. My mental slave master had me preaching for response --yelling, shouting, etc.-- and not for results like salvation, miracles and healing.

Today, ask yourself, "What has me bound?" Is it finances? Is it complacency? Or, the opinions of people? Are you living to please the master of your emotions and thoughts? Or, are you going after your dream to fulfil your God given purpose? Be free from toxic, destructive, negative thinking. Change your perception of your worth, and understand you are destined for greatness!! Oh, I have a new movie now, for myself. It is called "The Mindset Redemption," and It is a winner! Be Inspired Be Motivated to rewrite the story of your life today. Be Free and Live Free. -Christopher Brooks small voice that's saying "one more time" ring loud enough to make you Get Up and go after your dream!

Be Strong Saturday

"FOR THIS LIGHT MOMENTARY AFFLICTION IS PREPARING FOR US AN ETERNAL WEIGHT OF GLORY BEYOND ALL COMPARISON." **2 CORINTHIANS 4:17 ESV**

C.T. Fletcher is an American powerlifting vlogger, media personality, actor, personal trainer, and former powerlifter and bodybuilder. He is a three-time World Bench Press Champion and three-time World Strict Curl Champion. He speaks to his muscles while working out and commands his muscles to grow! He did not start, on day one, with the massive physique he proudly displays today. It took time and preparation. Preparation can be painful! To gain muscle mass, you must lift heavy weight. There is a tearing and breaking down of the muscle that happens to make room for growth.

You might be going through something in your life and do not understand the point of it all. Just know you're going through your preparation. This is a moment of tearing and breaking so there can be room for you to grow as a man, woman, entrepreneur, student, etc. Stop hanging with wimps and leeches who want the benefits of success, without making the necessary sacrifices to get there. Be the change, and surround yourself with strong, motivated, forward thinking people that are doers of greatness. Start your day from this day forward looking in the mirror and commanding yourself to be strong! Look at your business plan and command it to be strong! Any area of your life that needs to grow, tell it every day to be strong!

MOTIVATIONAL MOMENTS
PURSUING THE DREAM

Week Four

Be Secure Sunday

"BE CHEERFUL NO MATTER WHAT; PRAY ALL THE TIME; THANK GOD NO MATTER WHAT HAPPENS. THIS IS THE WAY GOD WANTS YOU WHO BELONG TO CHRIST JESUS TO LIVE." **1 THESSALONIANS 5:16-18 MSG**

My mother taught me how to pray. When I was very young, my mother's leg was hurting. I ran to her and began to pray for God to make it better. I was not even 10 years old at the time, but she told me God hears my prayers and I just believed.

When your life brings chaos, confusion, or painful moments you did not see coming, you must pray. Prayer will release healing and peace in the hard times. It gives you the strength you need to Be Resilient and get back up from those setbacks. Today be encouraged. Although you may have setbacks, you can bounce back by God's grace. We all have struggles. But those struggles do not define you or disqualify you from your purpose. Get up, brush your shoulders off, and with a heart of thanksgiving, keep pushing forward!

Be Motivated Monday

"THE [REVERENT] FEAR OF THE LORD [THAT IS, WORSHIPING HIM AND REGARDING HIM AS TRULY AWESOME] IS THE BEGINNING AND THE PREEMINENT PART OF KNOWLEDGE [ITS STARTING POINT AND ITS ESSENCE]; BUT ARROGANT FOOLS DESPISE [SKILLFUL AND GODLY] WISDOM AND INSTRUCTION AND SELF-DISCIPLINE." **PROVERBS 1:7 AMP**

My father would tell me when I was younger, "A fool and his money are soon parted". My mom would say things like, "If you do not listen you will feel". One of my brothers (you know who you are) would tell me, "Quit being dumb". Oh, how loving are my brother's words. Wisdom is the secret weapon of success that if received and applied, will give you results beyond your expectations. The book of Proverbs is a great place to focus for this week and attaining wisdom. It is my desire to see everyone that I encounter living their very best life; wisdom will definitely give you that life.

I do not always like what I am being told from my mentors, especially when it is something that makes me uncomfortable. A little discomfort today (sacrifice) will produce a huge harvest later (overflow). Be motivated today to seek those who walk in wisdom and open your heart and mind to receive wise instruction. It is going to make you ready for the blessing that is to come!

Be Truthful Tuesday

"BE SOBER, BE VIGILANT; BECAUSE YOUR ADVERSARY THE DEVIL WALKS ABOUT LIKE A ROARING LION, SEEKING WHOM HE MAY DEVOUR. RESIST HIM, STEADFAST IN THE FAITH, KNOWING THAT THE SAME SUFFERINGS ARE EXPERIENCED BY YOUR BROTHERHOOD IN THE WORLD." **1 PETER 5:8-9 NKJV**

There is an increasingly popular saying introduced to the world by the black lives matter movement that simply states, "Stay woke". These two words that have so much meaning and wisdom in them. While many use this phrase as a slang term or a punchline, its message of vigilance and awareness can lead you to a life of fulfillment. Sometimes, I find myself being so focused on challenges that come up in my business or frustrations of life, I forget to see the spiritual lessons God is teaching me. During the night, our home was burglarized and Tiffany's wallet was stolen. Nothing else was taken and no one was harmed. While we were doing our due diligence, God gave us peace through the ordeal. While the wallet was expensive, the lives of my family and my children's sense of security in their home is priceless. No chaos. No anger; just faith in God.

You are destined for greatness! Do not lose sight on your purpose when the unexpected comes, stay woke! The trials and tribulations of your life are spiritual. Be vigilant.

Be Wise Wednesday

"SO, WE MUST LISTEN VERY CAREFULLY TO THE TRUTH WE HAVE HEARD, OR WE MAY DRIFT AWAY FROM IT." **HEBREWS 2:1 NLT**

My mother used to tell me, "If you do not listen, you will feel". It meant that when you are given wise counsel, instructions from those who are over you or a lesson from which you are to learn, and do not pay attention to it or apply it, you will experience unnecessary challenges and hardships. Our lives can be rich and full of joy, success and purpose if we are willing to listen to the voice of wisdom that is found in the Word of God. Romans 10:17 reminds us that faith comes by hearing God's Word. It was my faith in God's Word that helped me through some of the toughest times in my life. After recently losing my cousin to cancer, being a victim to a robbery while we were asleep, and relocating to a new home, I remember mentors in the faith talking about God's faithfulness and I find strength in scriptures that speak of God's promises. Be wise and do not focus your thoughts on your struggles or failures but tune in to the promises of God. In His promises you will find strength, hope and peace.

Be Transparent Thursday

"ADAM AND HIS WIFE WERE BOTH NAKED, AND THEY FELT NO SHAME." **GENESIS 2:25 NIV**

Transparency is showing the true you. To hold your true self captive, in chains of fake smiles and empty conversation is a life of bondage and emotional torment. Until recently, I had this habit of only calling my parents and only talking about good stuff going on. I would talk to my mentor and only tell him about all the progress the B.E.Group was making.

Although what I was telling them was the truth, I still was lacking total honesty. I did not tell them I had such a horrific anxiety attack that I was moments from being hospitalized. I did not tell them I was struggling with the pressure of financing a business out of my own pocket while also maintaining a home. I only gave them the fluff. If you truly want to thrive in life and have healthy relationships and a successful ministry or business, you must find the strength to be transparent. I was highlighting the dream while hiding my personal nightmares. The freedom I have now came the day I realized my mentor is not just there to talk about success, but to be present when I am struggling emotionally, spiritually, financially, etc. I had to understand my father and mother are always proud of me, so I do not have to put that kind of pressure on myself to try to earn their love. Today declare, "My dream is real, my faith is strong, and today is my chance to be great!"

Be Free Friday

" 'COME,' SAID JESUS. THEN PETER GOT DOWN OUT OF THE BOAT, WALKED ON THE WATER, AND CAME TOWARD JESUS." **MATTHEW 14:29 NIV**

We all have had setbacks in our life. It might have been in relationships, in business or personal goals that did not work out the way you wanted. My desire is for you to be resilient and try again. Failure is part of the process to being great. Through failure, we learn and grow. The problem comes from holding on to the pain and shame of past failures. If you hold on to them, they will cripple your progress, and will become the voice in your head that makes you believe you are not smart enough, not good enough, and a list of other negative things to keep you limited.

You will never be truly satisfied in life until you begin to move into your God-given purpose. You might make a lot of money, have positions and titles. You can have the most beautiful woman or the most handsome man in your life, drive the newest vehicle and live in the largest house in your community. But, if you are not doing what you were created to do, there will always be that need for something more.

When I gave my first speech, as CEO of the B.E. Group, it was to a crowd that was totally different from any church I had ever spoken to in my twenty years of ministry. I felt like Peter. I was stepping out of the boat of comfort and preparation and walked on the waters of application. To "walk the walk and not just talk the talk" is not limited to doing right and wrong. It is moving from "I am going to do" to doing. Be free from that voice in your head and allow the Holy Spirit in your heart to lead you and guide you. You are not going to be great one day. You ARE great right now!

Be Strong Saturday

"LOOK TO THE LORD AND HIS STRENGTH; SEEK HIS FACE ALWAYS." **1 CHRONICLES 16:11 NIV**

I have learned that I am limited in my own strength. As strong of a woman as my wife is, there is also a point of limitation where even she can break. We all have a breaking point. But, why allow yourself to go that far. Through prayer, meditation and reading God's Word, you will find strength and encouragement during the difficult times. To be resilient, you must be honest with yourself, and acknowledge that you cannot travel the road to being great without God. Seek Him for wisdom and for direction in your journey.

I turned various difficult times or what could have been breaking points into opportunities. I went from being jobless to re-activating in the Army. I'm no longer suffering from PTSD, but an educator and voice of hope. I overcame the hurt and shame from divorce to having a loving marriage. Turn your breaking points into opportunities for God to Be Strong in you and through you!

Bible Verses by Week and Day

Week 1

Sunday: **Habakkuk 2:2-3 Message Bible**
Monday: **Proverbs 18:21 Message Bible**
Tuesday: **Proverbs 6:6-11 Message Bible**
Wednesday: **2 Chronicles 15:7 New International Version**
Thursday: **John 8:31-32 Message Bible**
Friday: **Psalm 119:71 Christian Standard Bible**
Saturday: **Habakkuk 2:3 King James Version**

Week 2

Sunday: **Hebrews 10:25 NLT**
Monday: **HEBREWS 12:1 AMP**
Tuesday: **Philippians 3:12 MSG**
Wednesday: **Proverbs 13:20 MSG**
Thursday: **Ephesians 4:25 NIV**
Friday: **2 Corinthians 5:17 AMP**
Saturday: **Luke 15:17-20 NIV**

Week 3

Sunday: **Habakkuk 2:2-3 MSG**
Monday: **Psalms 118:24 KJV**
Tuesday: **John 8:32 KJV**
Wednesday: **Philippians 1:25 NIV**
Thursday: **Romans 1:20 ESV**
Friday: **1 PETER 2:16 AMP**
Saturday: **2 Corinthians 4:17 ESV**

Week 4

Sunday: **1 Thessalonians 5:16-18 MSG**
Monday: **PROVERBS 1:7 AMP**
Tuesday: **1 Peter 5:8-9 NKJV**
Wednesday: **Hebrews 2:1 NLT**
Thursday: **Genesis 2:25 NIV**
Friday: **St. Mathew 14:29 NIV**
Saturday: **1 Chronicles 16:11 NIV**

About the Author

Elder Christopher Brooks is an international speaker, entrepreneur and ministry leader at Destiny Family Christian Center in El Paso. With twenty-six years of ministry experience, he has served as an associate pastor, evangelist, pastor of praise and worship, Christian education director, keynote speaker, and Bible teacher. As a prolific orator, Christopher delivers his sermons with humor, transparency and sound doctrine that transcends denominational barriers. Elder Brooks periodically hosts a local Christian television program, United with Christ on Life-TV. He also shares Motivational Moments on social media, sharing personal life lessons with biblical principles to help readers BE the best version of themselves.

. Chris is a retired infantry paratrooper with the United States Army. He is a graduate of Central Texas College and is a senior at New Mexico State University with a major in Communication Studies. He is a certified Professional Life Coach from the American Association of Christian Counselors, with a specialization in Transitional Coaching and is an active member of the Public Speakers Association and Toastmasters International.

For the past ten years, he has lived a joyful life with his wife, Tiffany along with their four children Chayil, Jeremiah, Chris Jr. and Alan.

Made in the USA
Middletown, DE
20 March 2019